Discovering Religions

Hinduism

FOUNDATION EDITION

SUE PENNEY

Heinemann Educational Publishers
Halley Court, Jordan Hill, Oxford OX2 8EJ
a division of Reed Educational & Professional Publishing Ltd

OXFORD MELBOURNE AUCKLAND
JOHANNESBURG BLANTYRE GABORONE
IBADAN PORTSMOUTH NH (US) CHICAGO

Heinemann is a registered trademark of Reed Educational & Professional Publishing
Ltd

03 02 01
10 9 8 7 6 5 4 3

British Library Cataloguing in Publication Data

ISBN 0 435 30472 0

Designed and typeset by Visual Image
Illustrated by Gecko Limited. Adapted into colour by Visual Image
Cover design by Keith Shaw at Threefold Design
Printed and bound in Great Britain by Bath Colourbooks, Glasgow

Acknowledgements

The publishers would like to thank the following for permission to use photographs:
The Ancient Art and Architecture Collection p. 8; Andes Press Agency p. 24;
Mohamed Ansar/Impact Photos pp. 32, 43; The Bridgeman Art Library p. 12; The J
Allan Cash Photo Library p. 27; Circa Photo Library pp. 17, 22, 29, 36, 40 (left);
Comstock p. 26; Douglas Dickens pp. 15, 20; C M Dixon p. 18; Ben Edwards/Impact
Photos p. 41; Sally and Richard Greenhill pp. 16, 44 (below), 45; Sunil
Gupta/Network p. 33; Ian Happs pp. 10, 19; Judy Harrison/Format Partners p. 34;
The Hutchinson Library pp. 28, 42, 47; Roshini Kempadoo/Format Partners p. 40
(right); Christine Osborne Pictures p. 6; Ann and Bury Peerless pp. 9, 11, 13, 14, 30,
31, 46; Sarita Sharma/Format Partners p. 44 (top); Topham Picturepoint pp. 21, 25,
35, 38, 39.

The publishers would like to thank Zefa for permission to reproduce the cover
photograph.

The publishers have made every effort to trace copyright holders. However, if any
material has been incorrectly acknowledged we would be pleased to correct this at
the earliest opportunity.

Contents

HINDUISM

WORSHIP

FESTIVALS

HISTORY

PEOPLE

MAP: where the main religions began

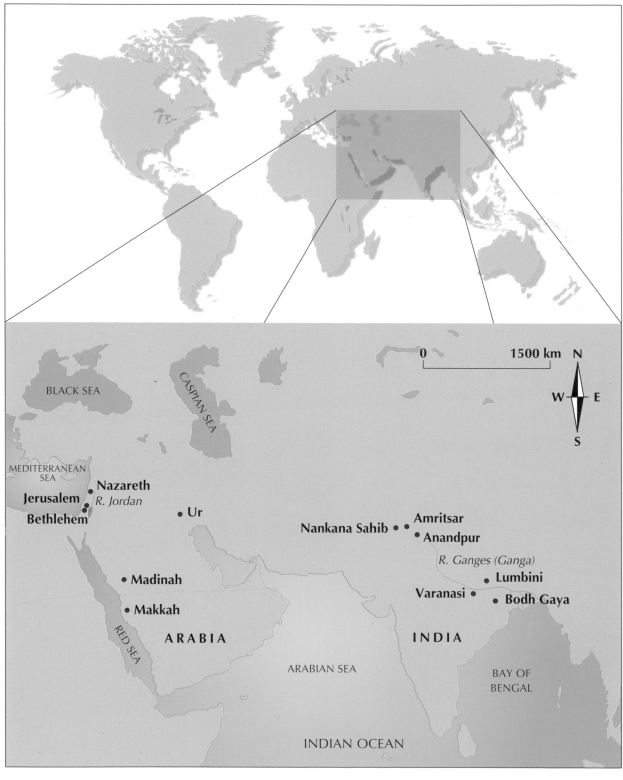

TIMECHART: when the main religions began

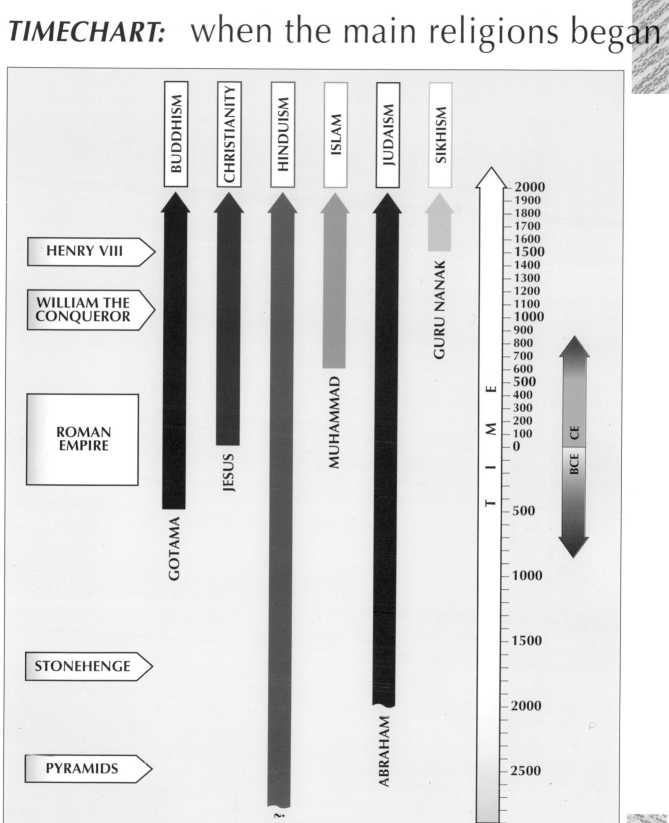

BUDDHISM	CHRISTIANITY	HINDUISM	ISLAM	JUDAISM	SIKHISM

GURU NANAK

HENRY VIII

WILLIAM THE
CONQUEROR

ROMAN
EMPIRE

MUHAMMAD

JESUS

GOTAMA

STONEHENGE

ABRAHAM

PYRAMIDS

TIME

BCE CE

2000
1900
1800
1700
1600
1500
1400
1300
1200
1100
1000
900
800
700
600
500
400
300
200
100
0
500
1000
1500
2000
2500

Note about dating systems   In this book dates are not called BC and AD which is the Christian dating system. The letters BCE and CE are used instead. BCE stands for 'Before the Common Era' and CE stands for 'Common Era'. BCE and CE can be used by people of all religions, Christians too. The year numbers are not changed.

Introducing Hinduism

This section tells you something about what Hindus believe.

When did Hinduism begin?

Hinduism is the oldest of the world's religions. No one really knows how old it is, but it goes back at least 5000 years. It began in the northern part of India. About 800 million people living in India are Hindus, and as many again live in other parts of the world. Over the years Hinduism has formed lots of different branches, and different Hindus may believe quite different things without being 'right' or 'wrong'.

What do Hindus believe?

Most Hindus do not call their religion Hinduism. They call it **Sanatan dharma**. This means '**eternal** truths'. Eternal means something that lasts forever. In other words, Hindus believe that their religion teaches things which have always been true and always will be. The truths are written about in the Hindu **holy** books. These are called the **Vedas** (see page 12). Most Hindus believe that the Vedas contain the most important part of their beliefs.

Hindus believe that there is one Great Power. Many Hindus would say that this power can be called God. The Hindu name for this power is **Brahman**. Most Hindus say that Brahman is not a person, and not male or female, but 'it'. Brahman is everywhere, and part of everything. Nothing would exist if Brahman was not in it. Hindus explain this by using an example. They say that it is like water with salt in it. The salt is there in even the tiniest drop of water, and it makes it what it is. In the same way, Brahman is in everything in the universe, and this makes everything what it is. Most Hindus say that Brahman can be seen through gods and goddesses. The three main gods are Shiva, Vishnu and Brahma (see pages 8–9).

Hindu children worshipping at home in London

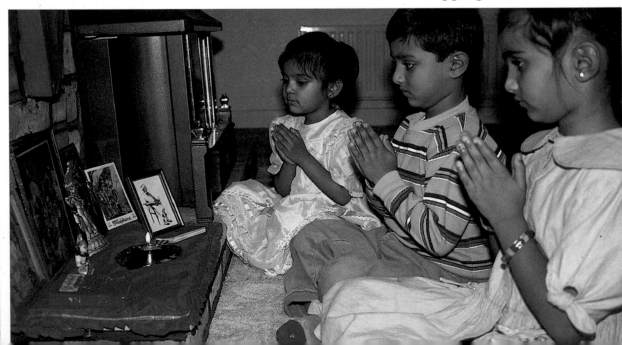

6

Reincarnation

Another important Hindu belief is **reincarnation**. Hindus believe that everything has a **soul**. A soul is a spirit, which lives on after the body has died. Hindus believe that when you die, your soul moves on to live in another person, or an animal or plant. Where it goes depends on how you have lived this life. Hindus aim to become good enough to break out of this cycle of birth and death, so that their soul can become part of Brahman. This will be perfect happiness.

Symbols which Hindus use

The **symbol** often used for Hinduism spells the world **Aum**. This is said as if it was spelt Ah-oo-m. Hindus believe this is a holy sound. They believe that it is a way of describing Brahman. All Hindu prayers begin with it.

The Hindu symbol 'Aum'

New words

Aum holy sound and symbol for Hindus

Brahman the Great Power

Eternal lasting forever

Holy to do with God

Reincarnation belief that a soul is reborn

Sanatan dharma eternal truths

Soul a person's spirit

Symbol something which stands for something else

Vedas Hindu holy books

Test yourself

How many people are Hindus?

What do Hindus call Hinduism?

What does Sanatan dharma mean?

What are the Vedas?

What are the three main gods called?

Think it through

1 Hinduism is thousands of years old and has millions of followers. How might this explain why not all Hindus believe exactly the same thing?

2 What is reincarnation? List three things which you think would be good and three things which you think would be bad about being reincarnated.

3 Why do Hindus use the sound Aum? Why do you think Hindu prayers begin with this sound?

Gods and goddesses 1

This section tells you about the most important gods in Hinduism.

There are thousands of gods and goddesses in Hinduism. When the religion began, people believed that the gods and goddesses really existed. Some Hindus probably still do believe this. However, most Hindus today believe that the gods are not real. They believe that they are symbols for describing Brahman. Human beings cannot understand Brahman, but the gods and goddesses are ways of showing what Brahman is like. Hindus believe that it easier to worship properly if they worship Brahman through a god or goddess they can understand.

The Trimurti

There are three gods who are most important in Hinduism. Many Hindus **worship** them. They are Brahma who makes things, Vishnu who **preserves** things and Shiva who destroys things. Hindus believe that these three gods work together in a pattern which never ends. Everything is made, lasts for a time, and is then destroyed. Together these three gods are called the **Trimurti**. This section concentrates on Vishnu and Shiva, as Brahma is not often worshipped today.

Vishnu

Vishnu is worshipped with several different names. This is because Hindus believe that he has come to earth nine times. Each time, he came to protect the earth because it was in danger. The two most important times were when he came as the god Rama, and when he came as the god Krishna. The story of Rama is in a long poem called the Ramayana (see page 15). Krishna's story is part of the poem called the Mahabharata (see page 14). Krishna is very important. He is worshipped by more Hindus than any other god is.

Shiva

Shiva is worshipped by about a quarter of all Hindus. He is the god who destroys, so he controls life and death. He is frightening

An old statue showing the Trimurti – Vishnu with Brahma and Shiva

Shiva, Lord of the Dance

because of his power, but Hindus also believe that he is kind. He destroys things that are old or no longer needed, but new things can only happen because old things are destroyed. He has at least four hands to show that he holds the power of life and death and good and evil. He is often shown dancing. One of his names is Lord of the Dance. His dance is the energy which keeps the universe moving. Sometimes the dance shows him destroying the monster, Ignorance.

New words

Preserve to keep things safe

Trimurti 'the three gods' – Brahma, Vishnu and Shiva

Worship show respect and love for a god

Test yourself

What does worship mean?

What is the Trimurti?

Where does the story of Rama appear?

Where does the story of Krishna appear?

What is another name for Shiva?

Think it through

1 Explain why Hindus worship gods and goddesses.

2 What is the pattern of life shown by the Trimurti? Why do Hindus believe this is so important?

3 Using the information on this page to help you, draw your own picture of Shiva as Lord of the Dance. Write a sentence explaining your drawing.

Gods and goddesses II

This section tells you about some popular Hindu gods and goddesses.

Choosing a god to worship

A Hindu can choose to worship any of the thousands of gods and goddesses. They usually choose one which their family worships, or one who they feel has helped them in some way.

Hindus do not believe that any one god or way of worship is better or worse than any other. They believe that the most important thing is that each person should worship God in the way that is right for them.

Many Hindu gods and goddesses have several different names to show different parts of their character. This can be quite confusing, even for Hindus. The important thing to remember is that all the gods and goddesses are ways of describing Brahman.

Shakti

Many of the gods have 'families'. Shakti is Shiva's wife. She is sometimes called the Mother Goddess. Like many gods and goddesses, she is sometimes fierce, sometimes kind and gentle. She has more than one name to show these different sides of her personality. In her fierce form

Kali

she is Kali, and is very frightening. Kali is often shown wearing a necklace of skulls, and with six or eight hands holding weapons. Shakti's kind and gentle side is called Parvati.

Lakshmi

Lakshmi is the wife of Vishnu. She is the goddess of beauty, wealth and good fortune. She is not as important as Shakti. Hindus often pray to her at New Year, asking for her help to make the year a good one.

Ganesha

Ganesha is the god of knowledge and strength. He has an elephant's head. In the god-family he is Shiva's son. The stories say that Shiva cut off Ganesha's head by mistake when he was in a temper. He gave him an elephant's head in its place. Ganesha is a very popular god, because many Hindus believe he can help solve problems.

Ganesha

Test yourself

How many gods can Hindus worship?

List three other names for Shakti.

What is Lakshmi the goddess of?

What is Ganesha the god of?

Why does Ganesha have an elephant's head?

Think it through

1 Why do the same gods and goddesses have different names? If you could choose two names to show different parts of your personality, what would they be?

2 Do you agree that everyone should worship in the way that is right for them?

3 Find out more about one of the gods or goddesses mentioned in this unit. Write a few sentences about them.

Holy books 1

This section tells you about the most important Hindu holy books.

Hinduism began thousands of years ago. In that time, many holy books have been written. Some praise the gods, some tell people how to worship, some are about Hindu beliefs. Most of the books are written in **Sanskrit**. This is one of the oldest languages in the world. Today, Sanskrit is only used in the religion. People do not use it to talk or write to one another. Some of the holy books are not often read today, but others are still very important.

The Vedas

The Vedas are the oldest of the Hindu holy books. They contain the basic truths which Hindus believe do not change. They go back to about 1200 BCE, but they were not written down for about 3000 years. The teachings were passed on when a father taught his son the words, the son then taught them to his son, and so on. In those days, not many people could read and write. This meant that people were used to learning things off by heart. It was the best way to remember them. The most important Veda is the first. It is called the Rig Veda. It contains over 1000 special poems.

The Upanishads

The Upanishads are the last part of each Veda. The name comes from Sanskrit words which mean 'sit down near'. This is how the Upanishads began. People sat down near wise men who were teaching about the Vedas, and learned from them. Eventually the wise men's teachings were written down. The Upanishads are about the most important things that Hindus believe, for example: what God is like, and how human beings can know God.

This page comes from an old copy of the Puranas. The writing is in Sanskrit

The Laws of Manu

Manu was a wise teacher whose teachings were written down in about 300 CE. The Laws of Manu tell Hindus about how they should live their lives. They also contain instructions for **priests**, the men who lead worship. Many Hindus try to obey all the Laws of Manu.

The Puranas

The word 'puranas' means 'olden times'. They are part of a group of books which help to explain the Vedas. They are mainly about the worship of the most important gods like Vishnu and Shiva. They contain many well known stories. Altogether, there are over half a million verses in the Puranas.

New words

Priests men who lead worship
Sanskrit very old language

Test yourself

What are the Vedas?

What is the Rig Veda?

Where are the Upanishads found?

What does Puranas mean?

Think it through

1 How were the Vedas remembered before they were written down? What would probably happen if people tried to remember something like that today? Give reasons for your answer.

2 What does Upanishad mean? How did the Upanishads begin?

3 Many of the holy books are very old. Why do you think Hindus believe that books written down thousands of years ago are still useful? What do you think?

Reading the holy books is an important part of Hindu worship

Holy books II

This section tells you about two important Hindu poems.

There are two very long poems which are part of the Hindu holy books. One is called the Mahabharata. The other is called the Ramayana.

The Mahabharata

The Mahabharata is the longest poem in the world. It has 100,000 verses! It was written by many different people over hundreds of years. The poem is complicated, because it has lots of different stories. They are included to teach lessons about the religion.

A painting showing Krishna and the prince before the battle (in Hinduism blue is a symbol for something holy)

The main story of the poem is about a quarrel between two royal families. They are cousins, and quarrel about who should be ruler of the country. One family tricks the other, and there is a great battle. Before the battle begins, one of the princes talks to the person driving his chariot. This person turns out to be the god Krishna in disguise. This is the most important part of the poem, and it includes the Bhagavad Gita.

The Bhagavad Gita

The Bhagavad Gita is probably the best-loved part of the Hindu holy books. The prince tells Krishna why he does not want to fight in the battle. Krishna teaches the prince about his duty and about the right ways for people to live and worship.

Dancing the Ramayana (Rama is facing Ravana, Hanuman is on the right)

The Ramayana

The Ramayana is not as long as the Mahabharata, but it still contains 24,000 verses. It was probably written down in about 100 CE. It tells the story of Prince Rama and his wife Sita. Prince Rama was an appearance of the god Vishnu.

In the story, Sita is kidnapped by a wicked monster called Ravana, who keeps her prisoner. Rama is helped by the monkey god Hanuman and his monkey army. Together they find Sita and rescue her. Rama kills Ravana and everything ends happily. Good wins over evil.

Why are the stories important?

Hindus believe that the stories in the Mahabharata and the Ramayana can be understood on many different levels. Children enjoy them because they are exciting stories. Adults realize that they also teach important lessons about the gods and the way to worship. The stories are an important part of Hindu life. Many Hindu actors and dancers use parts of the stories in their acts.

Test yourself

What are the two poems called?

How long is the Mahabharata?

Who does the prince talk to in the Bhagavad Gita?

Who kidnapped Sita?

Who helped Rama?

Think it through

1 Why do you think the Mahabharata was written by many different people over hundreds of years?

2 Explain why both adults and children can enjoy stories like the Mahabharata and the Ramayana.

3 How many reasons can you think of why Hindu actors and dancers use parts of these poems in their acts?

Worship I

This section tells you about how Hindus worship at home.

Hindus believe that their religion affects everything they do. They believe that God is in everything, so everything in their life can be worship. Cooking a meal or sweeping the floor can be worship if it is done properly and with care. Worship can also include repeating the names of God, reading the holy books and making offerings. The most common form of worship is called **puja**. This takes place in front of the **shrine** at home or in a temple.

Shrines

Temples and houses belonging to Hindus always have a shrine. This may be quite small and simple, or large and beautifully decorated. In a house, it may be just a shelf on a wall. If the family can afford it, the shrine may be in a room of its own. A shrine always has an **image** or picture of one or more of the gods or goddesses. They are surrounded by flowers and perfume.

Puja

Puja means making offerings to an image or picture of one of the gods or goddesses. Images and pictures help Hindus worship. They are ways of showing Brahman.

Puja can take place in many different ways. Some are very simple, others are very complicated.

Making puja

Worship takes place at least once a day. The point of worship is to spend time with God, so Hindus prepare for it very carefully. If there is an image in the shrine, it is washed and dried, and may have special coloured powders put on it. Gifts are offered, but they do not have to be large or expensive – a flower petal or a grain of rice is enough.

A Hindu woman making puja at home

While they are making puja, Hindus repeat verses from the holy books. They begin with the word Aum, which Hindus believe is a way of describing Brahman. Worshippers stand or sit cross-legged, and they do not wear shoes. They may put their hands together and touch their forehead, or they may kneel and touch the ground in front of the image with their forehead. These are all ways of showing respect.

Meditation

Meditation is an important part of Hindu worship. It is a way of training and controlling your mind. The aim is to think only about God, and to concentrate so completely that you empty your mind of all other thoughts. You stop being aware of

anything else, even yourself. There are instructions in the holy books for ways to meditate. In this book it is explained in more detail on page 24.

New words

Image special statue of a god in a shrine
Meditation controlling your mind so that you concentrate on God
Puja worship of a god or goddess
Shrine holy place

Test yourself

What is puja?

What is a shrine?

What is an image?

What is meditation?

Think it through

1 Why can every part of life be part of worship for a Hindu? Do you think this affects how they cook or clean?

2 Why do you think having a shrine in their house is important to Hindus?

3 Why do Hindus show so much respect to the image or picture in the shrine? Why do you think a grain of rice is enough for a gift?

This boy is praying in front of a shrine

Worship II

This section tells you about how Hindus worship in temples.

Temples

A **temple** is a special place that is used for worship. Hindus worship at home, too, but temple worship is special. Many Hindu temples are small and simple. Others are large and beautifully decorated with wooden carvings. Some of the more important temples are like small villages themselves. The proper name for a Hindu temple is a **mandir**.

All mandirs have at least one priest. His job is to look after the images. These can be of one god or goddess, or of many. Mandirs have a shrine room where the image is kept, and a room where the priest lives. Large mandirs have a main shrine room, and other rooms with shrines to gods who are not as important. There is always a river or other water so that people can wash before they worship. (This is a special washing to make them fit for worship. It has nothing to do with being dirty.)

Worship in a mandir

Worship begins before dawn, when the image of the god or goddess is 'woken up' by the priest. The priest says prayers, beginning with the word Aum. Then the image is washed and dried. It has special paste put on it, and may have flowers hung on it.

In a large mandir an image is kept in a sleeping room overnight. Each morning it is taken back to the shrine room. Then offerings are made to it. Worship may take place several times a day.

When worshippers arrive at the mandir, they take off their shoes to show respect. They give their gifts to the priest, who takes them into the shrine room. Ordinary people do not go into the shrine room except at

The main tower of an important mandir in India

18

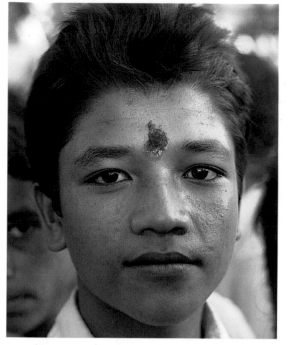

Tilak shows that the person has been to worship

festival time. The gifts are usually small. They may be money, but fruit and flowers are more common. Some worship includes **sacrificing** an animal, but this is not usual.

Havan and arti

Hindus do not usually worship in groups, but in large mandirs a priest may offer prayers in front of a group of people. There are hymns from the Vedas, and two forms of worship using fire. In **havan**, a small fire is lit in a special altar, and prayers are said as it burns. In **arti**, a tray of five lights is waved in front of the image, then carried among the people. They hold their hands over the flames, then wipe their hands over their head. They believe this means they can receive power from the god.

Tilak

During worship, people put a dot or stripes of special powder on their foreheads. This is called **tilak**. It shows that the person has been to worship. The shape shows which god they have worshipped. This is not the same as the red dot that many Hindu women wear on their foreheads, which shows that they are married.

New words

Arti worship using fire and lights
Havan worship by making offerings to the god of fire
Mandir Hindu temple
Sacrifice killing something so its life can be offered to a god
Temple building used for worship
Tilak powder placed on the forehead during worship

Test yourself

What is a temple?

What is the Hindu name for a temple?

What is a sacrifice?

What is tilak?

Think it through

1 Why do you think temple worship is special?

2 Explain why all mandirs have a priest living there. What does this show about the mandirs?

3 Explain how Hindus worship through fire. Why do they worship in this way?

Pilgrimage

This section tells you about some of the special places which Hindus visit.

A **pilgrimage** is a special journey which people make because of their religion. Many Hindus feel that going on a pilgrimage is an important part of their worship.

Places of pilgrimage

Most people go on a pilgrimage because they want to visit a special place. Often this is a place where the god they worship appeared to people, or has an important

The mandir at Puri

mandir. Sometimes they want to pray for something special, and believe their prayer is more likely to be answered if they are in a holy place.

Where do people go?

There are hundreds of places of pilgrimage all over India. Some may be only a day's journey, but many pilgrims take weeks or even months to walk to their chosen place of pilgrimage. Four mandirs are especially important. They are thousands of kilometres apart, at the four 'corners' of India. Puri is on the east coast, Dwarka is on the west coast, Badrinath is in the north. They are shrines to Vishnu. Rameshwaram on the south coast is a shrine to Shiva. Many Hindus spend almost all their lives saving up to visit them all. They believe that difficulties in getting there make the pilgrimage more worthwhile.

When pilgrims get to the mandir or shrine, they often crawl around it on their hands and knees. This shows that they are sorry for all the things they have done wrong. Worship at the shrines takes place in the same way as the people worship at home.

Holy rivers

Water is necessary for life, and Hindus respect many rivers. They believe the rivers are a symbol of God who gives life. Bathing in a holy river is important for Hindus. They believe it washes away **sin**. Sin means all the wrong things that a person has done in their life. There are seven holy rivers in India. The most famous is the Ganga (also called the Ganges). Hindus believe that

drinking even one drop of water from the River Ganga will wash away all their sins from this life and previous lives. Varanasi, the most holy city in India, is built on its banks.

Varanasi

Varanasi (sometimes called Benares) is where the Hindu stories say the god Shiva lived. Millions of people bathe in the River Ganga there. Special platforms called **ghats** beside the river allow people to bathe and make puja. The ghats are also where dead bodies are **cremated**. Every Hindu hopes to be in Varanasi when they die. Wherever they are, if they can, they arrange that after their body has been cremated, the ashes will be scattered on the River Ganga. They believe that this helps them to break out of the cycle of death and rebirth.

Worshippers bathing in the River Ganga at Varanasi

New words

Cremate burn a dead body
Ghats steps and platforms on a river bank
Pilgrimage special journey made because of someone's religion
Sin wrong things that a person has done

Test yourself

What is a pilgrimage?

What are ghats?

What does cremate mean?

Why are ashes scattered on the River Ganga?

Think it through

1 Why do you think that Hindus believe difficulties make a pilgrimage more worthwhile?

2 What is meant by sin? Why do you think crawling around a shrine on hands and knees is a way of showing you are sorry?

3 How would you feel about bathing in the River Ganga, or drinking its water? Why do you think millions of Hindus believe it is so important?

Hindu belief

This section tells you something about the beliefs that all Hindus would agree are the most important.

Dharma

Dharma means duty. Duty is something that you should do, but no one makes you do it. For Hindus, life involves a series of duties. Dharma is different for every person. It depends on your family, your job and many other things. It includes worshipping God, not hurting other people or animals, being honest and trustworthy, and doing your job as well as you can. Hindus believe that doing dharma well is very important.

Reincarnation

Reincarnation is the belief that your soul moves on to another being when you die.

Hindus call the soul the **atman**. They believe that the atman in everything is the same. So the atman of a plant, animal or human being is the same. They believe that the atman moves in a series of steps. It begins in plants and animals, and moves up to human beings. When someone dies, their atman moves on to another person. The repeated cycle of birth and death is called **samsara**. Whether you live a good or bad life decides what happens to your atman when you die.

Karma

Karma means action. It is the way Hindus explain how the atman moves from one being to another. A good karma in this life means a good life next time. A bad karma means a bad life next time. Part of this belief is that it is no good complaining if your life is hard, or boasting if your life is easy. It all depends on how you lived last time, so it is your own responsibility.

Hindus do not believe that you will be judged by God at the end of your life. This is not necessary, because the way you live decides whether your next life will be the same, or a step up or down. Some Hindus believe that a step can be missed if you have been very good or very bad. Some also believe that doing something very bad will mean your soul is reborn in an animal. Doing something very good may mean it is given a 'rest' before being reborn.

Part of dharma is doing your job as well as you can

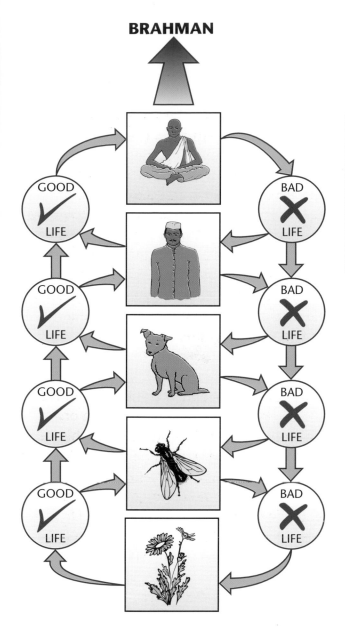

The law of samsara

New words

Atman the soul which is in everything
Dharma the duties of living
Karma the actions which affect rebirth
Moksha end of the rebirth cycle
Samsara the law of rebirth

Test yourself

What is dharma?

What do Hindus call the soul?

What is samsara?

What is karma?

What is moksha?

Think it through

1 What sort of things do you think are your duty? Choose three things, and write a sentence about each.

2 What do you think about the idea that the way you live now can affect a future life? How could this idea explain some of the world's problems?

3 Hindus say that moksha is like what happens when a river joins the sea. Is this a good description? Why?

Moksha

Moksha is the end of samsara. The atman breaks out of the death and rebirth cycle, and joins with Brahman. This can only happen when the atman is completely pure, and not affected by anything that happens on earth. Moksha is what every Hindu hopes to achieve.

Yogas

This section tells you about the different ways in which Hindus can break out of the cycle of birth and death.

Moksha is where the soul escapes from the cycle of birth and death and can join with Brahman. Hindus believe that there are four ways in which a person can achieve moksha: through knowledge, meditation, love and by doing your best in life. The four ways are called yogas. Yoga means a path. Anyone can use any of the paths, and people often follow different paths at different times in their life. Some paths are more difficult than others. Hindus believe that this does not matter, because different people have different abilities. What matters is that in the end you reach Brahman.

The path of knowledge

This does not mean knowing about a lot of things, it means knowing about the religion. Hindus who follow this path need a very good teacher. They must study the religion very carefully. They follow a pattern for their life. This means that they can learn more about the way that their soul (atman) fits in with God (Brahman).

The path of meditation

Meditation means controlling your mind so that you forget even yourself. The aim of meditation is to reach the 'real' you – the soul which is hidden in you. People who choose this path use special positions and exercises to help them concentrate. You can only follow this path if your life is free of things that might worry you. Thinking

Young Hindus in Britain learning about their religion

Meditation

about work, your home or your family would stop you concentrating. Ignoring them would go against Hindu teaching about your dharma. So you cannot follow this path unless you are free from responsibilities.

The path of love

This path means choosing a particular god or goddess and spending all your life worshipping them. Remember that Hindus believe that even something like cooking a meal is worship if you do it properly. Hindus following this path pray and make puja to the god or goddess, and go on pilgrimages to worship them. The god or goddess they worship is the most important thing in their life.

The path of doing your best

Many Hindus think that for ordinary people this is the best path. It means doing your dharma – your duty – as well as you possibly can. Dharma is different for everyone, so each person has to decide for themselves what this path means for them and then work hard to follow it.

Test yourself

How many ways are there in which a Hindu can achieve moksha?

What does yoga mean?

What is the aim of meditation?

Which path do most ordinary people follow?

Think it through

1 Why don't all Hindus follow the same path? Why do you think people follow different paths at different times in their life?

2 Why do you think most people choose to follow the path of doing your best?

3 Hindus often say that religion is like climbing a mountain – which path you follow is not important so long as you reach the top. Explain what you think this means. Do you agree with it?

Hindu life

This section tells you about two ways in which religion can affect a Hindu's life.

Hinduism teaches that there are four stages of life. They are called the four **ashramas**.

The student

The first stage is the student. From about the age of eight to twenty, young people should study and learn about the religion. They are then fit to go on to the second stage of life.

A sannyasin

The householder

The second stage is the householder. Householders are expected to work for their living, and marry and have a family.

The forest-dweller

When the family are grown up and the person is getting older – some people say about 50 years old – they should leave their home and friends. They should go and live on their own, in a quiet place. This stage is to learn to give up everything the person enjoys. They should concentrate only on their religion. It is a time to prepare for leaving the body behind when they die.

The holy man

The last stage, the **sannyasin**, is usually only taken by men. Sannyasin is the Hindu word for a holy man. It is quite common in India to see holy men sitting by the side of the road, teaching people. A sannyasin has no home. He usually has only the clothes he wears and a bowl for his food. He has given up all responsibilities, and can spend all his time thinking about his religion. You may understand this more easily if you look back at page 24.

Achieving moksha

Of course, not all Hindus live like this. Most young people cannot afford to spend twelve years studying the religion. Many do not want to give up their home and family when they get older. They stay in the second stage until they die. Hindus agree that it is the people who go on to the third and fourth stages who are most likely to break out of the cycle of death and rebirth.

Cows are allowed to wander where they like

Respecting all life

The Hindu belief in reincarnation means that Hindus respect all life. Many Hindus are vegetarian. They do not eat meat at all because they respect the life of animals. Even if they eat other sorts of meat, no Hindu will eat beef. This is because the cow is a **sacred** animal for Hindus. No one really knows the reason. It may be because the white cow is a symbol of atman – the soul which is present in everything. In India, cows are protected because they are sacred. They are milked, and their dung is used for fuel, but they are never killed for food. They are allowed to wander where they like, and there are severe punishments for killing a cow, even in an accident.

New words

Ashramas four stages of life for Hindus
Sacred to do with God
Sannyasin holy man

Test yourself

What do Hindus call the stages of life?

How long does the first stage of life last?

When does the third stage begin?

What is a sannyasin?

What is a white cow the symbol of?

Think it through

1 Write a sentence about each of the four stages of life which a Hindu may follow. Why do you think not all Hindus follow all of them?

2 What is the purpose of the third stage of life? What things do you think you would miss most if you were going to do this?

3 Explain what Hindus believe about cows. Why might they be so important?

Festivals I

This section tells you about the Hindu festival of Divali.

India is an enormous country. Festivals are often celebrated in different ways in different areas. Hindus living in other countries may celebrate them in a different way again. The same festival may remember quite different stories, depending on where it is being celebrated. For almost all Hindus, Divali is the most important festival of the year.

Divali

Divali takes place at the end of the Hindu month of Ashwin, so it is in October or November of the western calendar. In some places it lasts for three days, but, more usually, it lasts for five days. Divali means lights, and Hindus decorate their homes, mandirs and other important buildings with rows of lights. Years ago, small lamps made of clay were used. They were called divas, and this gives the festival its name. Today, Hindus usually use small electric lights.

Divali remembers several different stories. One of the most popular stories comes from the Ramayana (see page 15). It tells how Prince Rama won the battle against the wicked monster Ravana, and found his wife Sita. They returned home, and Rama became king. Lamps were lit all over the city to welcome Rama home. Other popular stories are about how the god Vishnu won a battle against a wicked giant, and how he tricked a king named Bali who was trying to take over the world.

Lighting candles for Divali

The goddess Lakshmi

A goddess is remembered at Divali, too. She is the goddess Lakshmi. Hindus believe that she brings good luck, especially for people who have shops or other businesses. She is supposed to visit houses which are clean and tidy. Some people think that the little lamps are to show her the way when she comes to visit.

Celebrating Divali

Divali is a festival which people celebrate with their families. They give each other presents and cards, and share meals with friends and relations. There are bonfires and fireworks, and singing and dancing. The idea is to show that darkness can be driven away by light. This shows that in the same way evil can be driven away by good.

Test yourself

When does Divali occur?

How long does the festival usually last?

What is a diva?

Who is the god most often remembered at Divali?

Who is the goddess remembered at Divali?

Think it through

1 Why do Hindus use lights at Divali?

2 Design a card which you could send to a Hindu friend at Divali.

3 Find out more about one of the stories of Divali. Work in groups and put together a poster or display.

Divali celebrations at a mandir in Britain

Festivals II

This section tells you about two Hindu festivals.

Janmashtami

Janmashtami celebrates the birthday of the god Krishna. Mandirs are specially decorated. So are shrines which have an image of the god Krishna. The stories about Krishna say that he was born at midnight, so many Hindus spend all night in the mandir. At midnight, there is singing and dancing. Then everyone shares sweets which have been specially cooked.

The most important story about Krishna is the Bhagavad Gita. It takes about three hours to read the Bhagavad Gita all the way through, and in many mandirs it is read out continuously for eight days and nights to celebrate the festival. The readings are timed so that they finish at midnight on Krishna's birthday.

An image of baby Krishna in a cradle

Navaratri

Navaratri means 'nine-nights', and this is the length of the festival. Most of the celebrations of Navaratri are to celebrate Shakti, the Mother Goddess (see page 10). She has many different names. At Navaratri she is Durga, a soldier who rides into battle on a lion. Anyone who worships Durga as their special goddess keeps this festival with great care. Durga is very fierce and frightening, but Hindus also believe she cares about people. She is the symbol of mothers.

In the story of the Ramayana, Prince Rama prays to Durga for help when his wife Sita has been kidnapped. So Navaratri is an important festival for families. Girls who have been married in the past year try to return home for this festival, and they are given presents. In northern India, there are plays in the open-air where parts of the story of the Ramayana are acted out.

Dassehra

Dassehra means 'tenth day'. It falls the day after the end of Navaratri. This is why Dassehra and Navaratri are sometimes put together as part of the same festival. At Dassehra, an image of the goddess Durga is taken to the nearest river and washed.

Hindus believe that as the image disappears under the water, it takes all their unhappiness and bad luck with it. This makes Dassehra a very happy festival.

The statue of Ravana at the Dassehra celebrations in New Delhi

Dassehra is also a time when Hindus remember the battle which Rama had with the wicked monster Ravana. There are bonfires, and statues of Ravana are burned. In New Delhi, the capital of India, there is always an enormous firework display. There are wooden statues 30 metres high of Ravana, his son and his brother. They are filled with fireworks and burned.

The story of Dassehra reminds people that good should overcome evil. It is a time when Hindus try to make up any quarrels which they may have had in the past year.

Test yourself

What is Krishna's birthday called?

How long do the readings from the Bhagavad Gita last?

What does Navaratri mean?

What does Dassehra mean?

Why do Hindus wash Durga in a river?

Think it through

1 Explain how Hindus celebrate Krishna's birth. Why do you think many Hindus go to the mandir?

2 Why is Navaratri an important festival for families?

3 Do you think having a special time for making up quarrels is a good idea? Give reasons for your answer.

Festivals III

This section tells you about other Hindu festivals.

Holi

Holi is a spring festival. It gets its name from Holika, a cruel princess who tried to kill a man who worshipped Vishnu. He did not die because he kept repeating the names of God. This reminds Hindus how important it is to trust God.

Many Hindus remember stories about when Krishna was young. He used to play tricks on people. Holi is a time for practical jokes. A favourite trick with children is to throw coloured powder and water at people walking along the streets. There are often water fights. It is a festival full of fun.

Raksha Bandhan

Raksha Bandhan takes place in July or August. At Raksha Bandhan, a girl ties a coloured silk or cotton bracelet around her brother's wrist. She hopes that it will protect him from danger, and it is a sign that he will protect her. This comes from a story about the god Indra. His wife had tied a magic string around his wrist and it saved him from an evil monster.

Ramnavami

Ramnavami is the birthday of the god Rama. It takes place in March or April. Rama is a very popular god, and many Hindus worship him. Those who normally worship at home usually make a special effort to worship at a mandir for Ramnavami. There are readings from the Ramayana. A special part of the worship is when they sing the Ramanama. This is a list of all the names of Rama. Many Hindus **fast** at Ramnavami.

For Hindus, fasting means going without certain foods. They do not eat foods like meat, fish, onions, garlic, wheat or rice.

Raksha Bandhan

Special patterns are part of the decorations at New Year

Foods like fresh fruit and milk are allowed. These are foods which many poor Hindu families cannot normally afford. Eating them is a way of helping to make the festival more special.

New Year

Hindus may celebrate New Year at different times, depending on where they live or where their families came from. Whenever they celebrate New Year it is always a chance to turn over a new leaf, and make changes in their life. Houses are cleaned or painted, and everyone wears new or clean clothes. Coloured chalks or powders are used to make patterns on the floor. These patterns are believed to bring good luck. Many people get up very early to make special puja at New Year.

New word

Fast go without food and drink for religious reasons

Test yourself

Where does the name Holi come from?

What is the Ramanama?

What is fasting?

What are New Year patterns supposed to bring?

Think it through

1 Why is Holi a time for practical jokes? Do you think you would enjoy joining in the festival?

2 Where does the custom of tying a bracelet around a brother's wrist come from? What is it a symbol of?

3 New Year is a time for making changes. Work in pairs to think of five changes you could each make in your life. Write a sentence about each of them.

Hindu history

This section tells you something about the history of Hinduism.

The beginnings of Hinduism

No one knows exactly when Hinduism began, but it was at least 5000 years ago. It began gradually among people who lived in the north of the country we now call India. They worshipped gods in the things they saw around them. They were gods of fire, water and wind. Then the country was taken over by people from the country we call Iran. They worshipped gods of the sun, moon and stars.

As the years passed, these two sorts of worship joined together. People did not stop worshipping their own gods, but they began to worship other ones as well. Gradually people began to believe that these different gods were really all ways of looking at Brahman, the Great Power.

Hinduism and Buddhism

Buddhists follow the teachings of Gotama, the Buddha. He lived in India in the fifth century BCE. Many people who had been Hindus began to follow the teachings of the Buddha. In the third century BCE, India was ruled by an Emperor called Asoka. He became a Buddhist, and helped to spread the teachings of Buddhism. By the end of the century, almost everyone living in India was Buddhist.

Hindu teachers realized that if it was going to survive, Hinduism needed to be more organized. They began to write down the Vedas and the great poems. They spent a lot of time teaching, and people began to learn the lessons behind the stories. More people began to follow Hinduism again.

Hinduism and Islam

After about 1100 CE, **Muslims** ruled India for about 300 years. Muslims follow the religion of Islam. Many people left Hinduism and became Muslim. Muslims did not like the way Hindus worshipped, and many Hindu temples were pulled down. Hinduism became less popular again.

Havan (offerings to the god of fire) is part of Hindu worship today

Muslims moving to Pakistan crowd onto a train in 1947

In the nineteenth century, British people ruled India. This was a time when the world was changing very quickly. Hinduism had to show that it was still important in the changing world. Many famous Hindu teachers worked hard to show that Hinduism was an important world religion.

Independence

India became independent of British rule in 1947. The country was divided. A new country called Pakistan was created, to be a Muslim country. Thousands of Hindus living in that area moved back to India. Thousands of Muslims living in India moved to the new country of Pakistan. It was a time of great suffering. There were riots in many places, and thousands of people were killed. Since that time, most people living in India have been Hindus.

Hinduism accepts many different views. Hindus say that all religions are a search for truth. What matters is that people find the truth for themselves.

New words

Buddhists followers of Gotama Buddha
Muslims followers of the religion of Islam

Test yourself

Whose teachings do Buddhists follow?

Who was Asoka?

What is a Muslim?

When did India become independent?

Which new country was created?

Think it through

1 Why do you think that people thousands of years ago thought that there were gods in fire and water, or the sun and moon?

2 What were the problems caused by making the new country of Pakistan? What reasons can you think of why so many people were unhappy about the changes?

3 Work in small groups to make up a conversation or a short play to show that you believe something far more if you have found it out for yourself.

The caste system

This section tells you about the different groups of people in India.

Different people are good at different things. Hinduism teaches that this is mainly because of their previous lives. The teaching about dharma tells Hindus that they should make the most of their abilities. This led to the idea that some groups of people were good at particular things. For hundreds of years, Hindus have been divided into groups, according to their job. These groups are called **varnas**.

The four varnas

There are four groups or varnas. The most important group are **Brahmins**. They are priests. The second group are **Kshatriyas**. They are soldiers. The third group are **Vaishyas**. They are shop-keepers and farmers. The fourth group are **Shudras**. They are servants for the other three groups. Below these four groups are the **Harijans**, the **untouchables**.

These four main groups gradually divided into many smaller groups. The smaller groups are called **jatis** or **castes**. Your jati depends on the jati of your family. Some jatis are 'higher' or 'lower' than other jatis. People used to be very strict about not having anything to do with people who came from a lower jati than their own. For example, people would only marry someone from the same jati, and they would not eat food prepared by someone from a lower jati. Some people are still very strict about this.

Harijans

The lowest group of people in Hinduism are the Harijans. They are below the other four groups. They do the dirtiest jobs.

For hundreds of years, other Hindus would not have anything to do with Harijans. They

Priests are usually Brahmins

called them 'untouchables'. In the early years of the twentieth century, the Hindu leader Gandhi worked hard to improve the lives of untouchables. He gave them the name Harijans. This means 'children of God'.

Changing the caste system

This way of dividing people into groups is called the caste system. It is the way that people in India have lived for hundreds of years. In the last 50 years, things have changed. People do jobs outside their varna. People who live and work in cities cannot be so careful about who they meet or talk to. In factories and shops, they have to meet and talk to people who are not from their own group. The rules about jatis cannot be kept so strictly.

Now many Brahmins are not priests, and not everyone in the army is a Kshatriya. Many people who own shops are not Vaishyas. Brahmins and Harijans are most likely to be interested in what varna they

belong to. However, most people still know what jati they belong to, and what this means to other people. Since 1947, it has been against the law in India to treat former untouchables differently. However, it takes a long time to change the way people think. In many villages in India, the caste system is still kept very strictly.

New words

Brahmins first varna
Castes another name for jatis
Harijans 'children of God' – untouchables
Jatis parts of a varna
Kshatriyas second varna
Shudras fourth varna
Untouchables lowest group of people
Vaishyas third varna
Varnas the four main groups of Hindu people

Test yourself

What are the four varnas?

What is the first varna?

What is the fourth varna?

What is a jati?

What does Harijan mean?

Think it through

1 Why do you think Gandhi chose to call untouchables 'children of God'? What do you think he was trying to achieve?

2 Why do you think Brahmins and Harijans are likely to be the most aware of which varna they belong to?

3 What do you think about people being treated differently because of their background? Work in pairs to discuss what you would do if you felt that this was happening to a friend of yours.

Mahatma Gandhi

This section tells you about one of the most important Hindus in the last hundred years.

Gandhi's early life

Mohandas Gandhi was born in 1869 in a small town in India. He was a shy, quiet child. When he was thirteen, his parents arranged for him to marry a girl called Kasturbai. In those days, children quite often got married. At first he and his wife did not get on very well. When they grew up, they became very close.

Gandhi and his wife in 1913

When Gandhi was sixteen, his father died. The family were short of money, and Gandhi needed to earn his living. A friend suggested he should go to England and study law. At first his family thought this was impossible, but Gandhi persuaded them. His wife sold her jewellery to buy his ticket.

Gandhi in South Africa

When he passed his exams in 1891, Gandhi went back to India. He found it hard to get a job, and he was offered work in South Africa. When he was there, he realized that brown and black skinned people were being treated unfairly. Treating someone unfairly because of their background is called **discrimination**.

When Gandhi's law work was finished, he decided to stay in Africa to try to improve the way Indians were being treated. He became a fighter for freedom. He did not fight in the same way as other people. He said that using violence to get what you want was wrong. He talked about **ahimsa**. This means fighting without using violence. He said that you should stand up for what you believe, but your fighting should be peaceful.

Gandhi's work in India

Gandhi went back to India in 1915. By this time, he was very well known. An Indian poet called him 'Great Soul', and for the rest of his life Gandhi was known by the Indian word for this – **Mahatma**. He began working to improve the lives of the untouchables (see page 37).

Gandhi's body
was surrounded
by rose petals

When India was becoming independent from Britain, Gandhi played an important part in the talks. He did his best to calm the fighting between Hindus and Muslims when the new country of Pakistan was made in 1947. This made him some enemies. Some people felt that Pakistan should never have been made. They felt this so strongly that they believed they should fight to get the land back. They knew that Gandhi would never agree, so they decided they had to get rid of him.

On 30 January 1948, Gandhi was talking to a large crowd in Delhi when a gunman in the crowd fired at him. He was shot three times, and died at once. His funeral took place the next day, and over three million people took part in his funeral procession.

Today, Mahatma Gandhi is remembered and respected as a man of peace not only by Hindus, but by people all over the world.

Test yourself

When was Gandhi born?

What is discrimination?

What is ahimsa?

What does Mahatma mean?

Think it through

1 Do you think it is possible to stand up for what you believe without fighting? Discuss your ideas in pairs, then write about what the advantages and disadvantages would be.

2 What do you think calling someone 'Great Soul' means? What does it tell you about Gandhi?

3 Work in groups on a project about the life of Gandhi. How did he show the teachings of Hinduism in his life?

New words

Ahimsa fighting for what you believe without using violence
Discrimination treating someone unfairly because of their background
Mahatma 'Great Soul' (title for Gandhi)

Hindus in Britain

This section tells you something about Hindus who live in Britain.

In 1997 there were about 360,000 Hindus living in Britain. Most come from families who have moved to Britain from India in the last 50 years. After World War II, British industries were short of workers. People from many countries were encouraged to come to Britain to work. Of course, they brought their religions with them.

Worship in mandirs

In India, worship as part of a group does not happen very often, except at important mandirs. In countries where most people are not Hindu, meeting with people who share the same religion and background is very important. Hindus have started meeting together for worship. Usually worship takes place on a Sunday, because this fits into the British way of life.

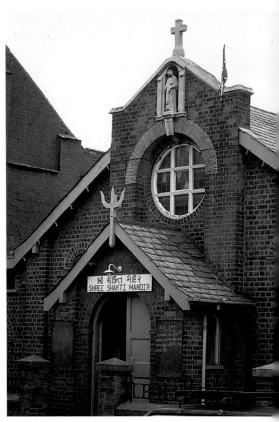

Many Hindu mandirs in Britain are in buildings that have been altered

There are about 150 Hindu mandirs in Britain. Most are in buildings which were built to be something else, because building a new mandir is very expensive. Most mandirs in Britain are dedicated to Krishna or Rama.

Worship in the home

Wherever Hindus live, the most important worship takes place in their home. This is even more important in countries where most people are not Hindu. Children learn about the religion mainly from what they are taught at home. All Hindu homes have a shrine. If the family can afford it, the shrine is in a separate room. If not, it may be just a shelf in the kitchen or a bedroom. Family worship takes place there in exactly the same way as it does in India.

Inside a Hindu mandir in Preston

Joining Hinduism

Hindus do not encourage people to **convert** to Hinduism. They believe that each person should find out the truth for themselves, and follow it. However, many people in other countries have been impressed by Hindu teachings. A Hindu teacher is often called a **guru** or a **swami**.

Hare Krishna

Some gurus have groups of followers. These followers try to carry out the teachings of the guru in their lives. Many Hindus believe that meditating on the teachings of a guru will help them to avoid being reborn again. A well known modern guru is Swami Prabhupada. He began the group called International Society for Krishna Consciousness in 1967. This group is often called Hare Krishna, because its followers meditate on the name of Krishna. All its temples are run by people who have converted to Hinduism. There are members of the group in many British cities, easily recognized by the yellow robes they wear.

A Hare Krishna procession in London

New words

Convert to become a member of a religion
Guru religious teacher
Swami title for some Hindu holy mer

Test yourself

When do Hindus in Britain usually meet for worship?

What does convert mean?

What is a guru?

What is a swami?

Who began the Hare Krishna movement?

Think it through

1 Why do Hindus in Britain meet for worship? What other reasons are there why such meetings might be important?

2 What do Hindus feel about trying to convert people to a religion?

3 If possible, invite a Hindu to come and talk to your group about their life and what they believe. Remember to prepare some questions in advance!

Special occasions 1

This section tells you about important things which happen to young Hindus.

Samskars

The special ceremonies in a Hindu's life are called **samskars**. Altogether there are sixteen samskars, which mark important events in a person's life. The correct way to perform them is written in the holy books.

Before birth

The first three samskars happen before a child is even born. They are prayers asking God to protect the mother and the baby, so that the child will be born healthy.

Birth

When the baby is born, he or she is washed. Then the baby's father places a few drops of honey and **ghee** in their mouth, using a gold ring. Then he says a prayer from the holy books. This is the fourth samskar.

Most Hindus take a careful note of the exact time and place that a baby is born. This information will be used by the priest who prepares the baby's horoscope. A horoscope is a way of telling the future based on the position of the stars. Many Hindus use horoscopes to work out the best time for important events in their life to take place.

The naming ceremony

A Hindu baby is usually given its name when it is twelve days old. This is the fifth samskar. Hindus believe that choosing the right name is very important. A priest is asked to suggest the first letter or a sound from which the name is chosen. Friends and relations come to the baby's house. The baby is dressed in new clothes, and placed in a cradle.

The ceremony itself is very simple. The eldest woman in the family says what the baby's name is going to be. The father whispers in its ear, 'Now your name is...' There are songs, and everyone eats a sweet made of fruit, nuts and sugar.

The first hair cut

As the child grows up, there are three more samskars. The most important is the ninth samskar, which is his or her first hair cut. It usually takes place when the baby is just over a year old. For a boy this means having his whole head shaved. It is a way of showing that any bad karma from his previous life has been taken away.

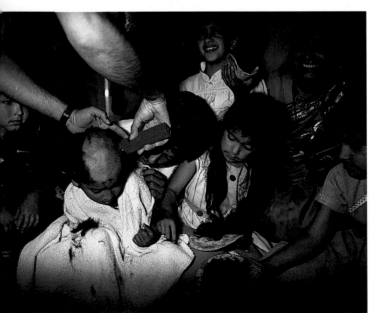

Shaving a boy's head is the ninth samskar

 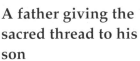

A father giving the sacred thread to his son

The thread ceremony

This is the tenth samskar, and only happens to boys of the three higher varnas. It is a very important ceremony because it is the time when he joins the religion. It marks his 'birth' into the religion, so it is the reason why the three higher varnas are sometimes called the 'twice born'.

The boy is usually aged between seven and twelve. He prepares for the ceremony with the help of a guru, who becomes his teacher afterwards. The sacred thread – a special loop of cotton – is hung over the boy's left shoulder. It hangs down to his right hip. Once he has been given this thread, a boy is counted as a man. He can read the Vedas and take part in ceremonies to do with the religion. He wears it all the time for the rest of his life, changing it at festivals.

New words

Ghee purified butter
Samskars ceremonies which mark a stage of life

Test yourself

What is a samskar?

How many samskars are there?

When is a Hindu baby given its name?

What is the sacred thread?

Think it through

1 What is a horoscope? Do you think the stars can tell you anything about your life?

2 Why do you think a priest is often asked to suggest the first letter for the baby's name?

3 Is it a good idea to have ceremonies to mark stages in life? How do you think a boy feels before the thread ceremony? How do you think he feels afterwards?

Special occasions II

This section tells you about Hindu weddings.

Arranged marriages

Hindus think that marriage is important, so that there can be children to carry on the family. Parents usually help their children choose a suitable person to marry. This is called an **arranged marriage**. In the past, couples did not meet until their wedding day, but today things are not usually so strict. The young people may suggest someone suitable, or at least have met a few times before the wedding.

The wedding

A Hindu marriage ceremony lasts about an hour, but the celebrations may go on for several days. The ceremony takes place in a mandir or in the bride's home. She wears special make-up, and a dye is used to make special patterns on her hands and feet. She wears a new red and gold **sari**, and lots of gold jewellery.

The bridegroom arrives first, and the bride's father welcomes him. When the bride arrives, she is wearing a veil. She takes this off during the ceremony. The couple sit next to each other under a decorated canopy. They sit in front of a special fire. Their right hands are tied together, and water is sprinkled on them. The bride's father 'gives' her to the bridegroom. There are prayers and offerings of rice.

The most important part of the marriage is when the couple take seven steps together. They walk towards the fire. At each step,

A Hindu bride wears beautiful jewellery

they stop and make promises to each other. While they do this, they are joined by a piece of cloth like a scarf. It is hung round the bridegroom's neck and tied to the bride's sari. This is a symbol that they are being joined as husband and wife.

The couple's right hands are tied together

The couple sit together under a special canopy

Once they have taken the steps together, they are married. There are more prayers and readings. People throw flower petals before they give the couple wedding presents. Then everyone shares a meal. After she is married, a woman is counted as belonging to her husband's family.

Divorce

The law in India allows divorce, but strict Hindus think marriage should only be ended when the husband or wife dies. It is a disgrace to both families if the marriage ends in divorce.

New words

Arranged marriage marriage where a partner is chosen or suggested by relations

Sari long piece of cloth worn as a dress

Test yourself

What is an arranged marriage?

What colour is a Hindu bride's sari?

Where do the couple sit?

How many steps do the couple take together?

What do strict Hindus feel about divorce?

Think it through

1 Think of three advantages and three disadvantages of an arranged marriage.

2 What is the most important part of the ceremony? Why are the couple joined together by the scarf while they make the promises?

3 Design a wedding card for a Hindu couple who are getting married.

Special occasions III

This section tells you about what happens when a Hindu dies.

Hindus believe in rebirth, so they do not think that death is the end. It is seen as being a welcome release from life. Of course, people are sad because the person they loved is no longer with them, but funerals are a time for looking forward, too. It is the custom for Hindu funerals to be on the day after death.

A Hindu funeral

When someone dies, their body is washed and placed in a special cloth called a **shroud**. The body has flowers put on it, then it is carried on a special stretcher to be cremated.

If possible, the body is cremated by one of the sacred rivers in India. The special platforms called ghats by the rivers are used for cremations. The body is placed on a special fire called a **funeral pyre**. It is made of wood, with ghee to help it burn. Sometimes blocks of sandalwood are included in the pyre, which burn with a sweet smell.

The eldest son or, if there is no son, another close relative, walks around the pyre carrying a lighted torch. He uses this to set fire to the wood. There are special prayers and readings from the holy books. They remind the people that everyone who dies will be reborn. It is the duty of the eldest son to remain at the fire until it has gone out, when he collects the ashes.

In Indian cities, and in countries where bodies cannot be burned in the open air, they are taken to a **crematorium**. Important customs like walking around the body with a lighted torch are carried out at the undertakers. The ashes are collected after the body has been cremated.

A Hindu funeral arriving at the place for cremation

Funeral ghats on
the banks of the
River Ganga at
Varanasi

Many Hindus have the ashes of their
relatives taken to the city of Varanasi to be
scattered on the River Ganga, because they
believe that this will save the person many
future rebirths.

The kriya ceremony

The **kriya ceremony** takes place ten or
twelve days after the funeral. Rice and milk
are made into offerings, not just for the
person who has died, but for everyone in
the family who has died in the past. Once
this ceremony has been held, Hindus
believe that the person's soul has found
another body, and the family can return to
living their normal life.

New words

Crematorium place where dead
  bodies are burned
Funeral pyre pile of wood for burning
  a body
Kriya ceremony final ceremony after
  a death
Shroud piece of cloth in which a
  dead body is wrapped

Test yourself

What is a dead body wrapped in?

What is the fire called?

What is a crematorium?

Where are many ashes scattered?

When is the kriya ceremony held?

Think it through

1 Why is death a time of hope for
Hindus, as well as of sadness?

2 Why do relatives often take a lot of
trouble to make sure that someone's
ashes are scattered on the River
Ganga?

3 What does the kriya ceremony
involve? How do you think the
relatives feel when they perform
this ceremony?

Glossary

The page numbers tell you where you can find out most about these words.

Ahimsa fighting for what you believe without using violence page 38

Arranged marriage marriage where a partner is chosen or suggested by relations page 44

Arti worship using fire and lights page 19

Ashramas four stages of life for Hindus page 26

Atman the soul which is in everything page 22

Aum holy sound and symbol for Hindus page 7

Brahman the Great Power page 6

Brahmins first varna page 36

Buddhists followers of Gotama Buddha page 34

Castes another name for jatis page 36

Convert to become a member of a religion page 41

Cremate burn a dead body page 21

Crematorium place where dead bodies are burned page 46

Dharma the duties of living page 22

Discrimination treating someone unfairly because of their background page 38

Eternal lasting forever page 6

Fast go without food and drink for religious reasons page 32

Funeral pyre pile of wood for burning a body page 46

Ghats steps and platforms on a river bank page 21

Ghee purified butter page 42

Guru religious teacher page 41

Harijans 'children of God' – untouchables page 36

Havan worship by making offerings to the god of fire page 19

Holy to do with God page 6

Image special statue of a god in a shrine page 16

Jatis parts of a varna page 36

Karma the actions which affect rebirth page 22

Kriya ceremony final ceremony after a death page 47

Kshatriyas second varna page 36

Mahatma 'Great Soul' (title for Gandhi) page 38

Mandir Hindu temple page 18

Meditation controlling your mind so that you can concentrate on God page 17

Moksha the end of the rebirth cycle page 23

Muslims followers of the religion of Islam page 34

Pilgrimage special journey made because of someone's religion page 20

Preserve to keep things safe page 8

Priests men who lead worship page 13

Puja worship of a god or goddess page 16

Reincarnation belief that a soul is reborn page 7

Sacred to do with God page 27

Sacrifice killing something so its life can be offered to a god page 19

Samsara the law of rebirth page 22

Samskars ceremonies which mark a stage of life page 42

Sanatan dharma eternal truths page 6

Sannyasin holy man page 26

Sanskrit very old language page 12

Sari long piece of cloth worn as a dress page 45

Shrine holy place page 16

Shroud piece of cloth in which a dead body is wrapped page 46

Shudras fourth varna page 36

Sin wrong things that a person has done page 20

Soul a person's spirit page 7

Swami title for some Hindu holy men page 41

Symbol something that stands for something else page 7

Temple building used for worship page 18

Tilak powder placed on the forehead during worship page 19

Trimurti 'the three gods' – Brahma, Vishnu and Shiva page 8

Untouchables lowest group of people page 36

Vaishyas third varna page 36

Varnas the four main groups of Hindu people page 36

Vedas Hindu holy books page 6

Worship show respect and love for a god page 8